Sports and Society

Scott Witmer

Heinemann Library
Chicago, Illinois

www.capstonepub.com
Visit our website to find out
more information about
Heinemann-Raintree books.

To order:

☎ Phone 800-747-4992

▣ Visit www.capstonepub.com
to browse our catalog and order online.

Edited by Adrian Vigliano and Claire Throp
Designed by Richard Parker
Picture research by Ruth Blair
Originated by Capstone Global Library Ltd
Printed in the United States of America in North
Mankato, Minnesota. 022013   007200RP

15 14 13
10 9 8 7 6 5 4 3

Library of Congress Cataloging-in-Publication Data
Witmer, Scott.
  Sports and society / Scott Witmer.
    p. cm.—(Ethics of sports)
  Includes bibliographical references and index.
  ISBN 978-1-4329-5979-1 (hb)—ISBN 978-1-4329-
5984-5 (pb) 1. Sports—Sociological aspects. I. Title.
  GV706.5.W58 2012
  306.483—dc22   2011014610

Acknowledgments
We would like to thank the following for permission to
reproduce photographs: Corbis pp. 4 (© Joseph Sohm/
Visions of America), 7 (© David Turnley), 17 (© Jon
Hicks), 19 (© Paulo Fridman), 20 (© Andres Kudacki),
27 (© Adam Stoltman), 30 (© Bettmann), 33 (© David
Gray/Reuters), 34 (© Fabrizio Bensch/Reuters), 36 (©
Hulton-Deutsch Collection), 43 (© Leo Mason), 45 (©
Race-Press.com/dpa), 47 (© Matthew Ashton/AMA);
Getty Images pp. 8 (Michael Steele), 15 (Olivier Morin/
AFP), 28 (Ben Stansall/AFP), 32 (Jamie McDonald), 39
(Tom Pennington), 40 (Andreas Rentz/Bongarts), 51
(Bob Thomas); Shutterstock pp. 5 (© Robert J. Beyers
II), 11 (© MAT), 13 (© EcoPrint), 22 (© J. Henning
Buchholz), 24 (© Iurii Osadchi), 49 (© fstockfoto), 52
(© Zoran Karapancev).

Cover photograph of a matador reproduced with
permission of Corbis (© Marcelo del Pozo/Reuters).

We would like to thank Shawn E. Klein for his
invaluable help in the preparation of this book.

Every effort has been made to contact copyright holders
of any material reproduced in this book. Any omissions
will be rectified in subsequent printings if notice is
given to the publisher.

Disclaimer
All the Internet addresses (URLs) given in this book
were valid at the time of going to press. However, due to
the dynamic nature of the Internet, some addresses may
have changed, or sites may have changed or ceased to
exist since publication. While the author and publisher
regret any inconvenience this may cause readers, no
responsibility for any such changes can be accepted by
either the author or the publisher.

CONTENTS

Some words are printed in bold, **like this**. You can find out what they mean by looking in the glossary.

SPORTS CULTURE AND SOCIOLOGY

The thrill of sports is well known to players and fans in every part of the world. It can be felt in the moment of anticipation shared by a stadium of spectators as an Olympic ski jumper launches into the air, or in the energy exhausted during a game of soccer in the neighborhood streets of a small town in Argentina. Almost everyone in the world has experienced the physical and emotional excitement of sports. But why are sports so popular in different societies around the world? Are sports just fun and games, or do they fulfill deeper needs?

Throughout history, sports have been an element of **culture**, the shared values and lifestyle characteristics of a society. Like other cultural activities such as art and music, sports are an important part of human social life. By looking at sports through the lens of **sociology**, the study and interpretation of human social behavior, we can understand how sports function in society, and why they appeal to different cultures in different ways.

Baseball fans at Dodger Stadium in Los Angeles support their team during the 2008 National League Championship Series. For spectators, excitement is an important part of the experience of sports.

Amateur athletes play soccer for fun and **recreation**. People take part in amateur sports for many different reasons.

Sports and society

Because sports are considered a fun distraction from the serious responsibilities of everyday life, the real-world effects of sports culture are often ignored. Many people consider sports to be entertainment or innocent enjoyment. But they do not realize that social problems such as violence and **prejudice** can also be a part of sports culture.[1]

This book will consider the role of **ethics** in sports, examining issues of right and wrong as they relate to human behavior. **Ethical** considerations help members of society to define ways to live that are fair to others and that allow society to function. We will see how sports culture shapes and reinforces ideas about how we relate to one another.

What are sports?

Why are certain activities considered sports, while others are not? What qualities make something a sport? Which of the following do you think are sports, and why? Look back to see if your opinion changes after you read this book:

- auto racing
- bowling
- bullfighting
- foxhunting
- golf

- gymnastics
- ice dancing
- long-distance running
- mountain climbing
- surfing

EARLY SPORTS: FROM PLAY TO WAR

What are the most important elements of sports? People define sports in different ways—as exercise, as physical skills, or as social activities to be enjoyed with friends. Many **sociologists** consider the concept of "play" to be the most important element of sports.

Play-based activity has been a part of human social life for as long as culture has existed.[1] Scientists have discovered evidence of play that resembles sports dating as far back as 3500 BCE. Although they were not known as sports at the time, some of the earliest sportlike activities played by ancient cultures included wrestling, acrobatics, hunting, running, and various types of ball games.[2]

What is play?

Play is at the heart of sports, but what is play exactly? Loosely defined, play is any activity pursued for its own enjoyment. In other words, it is something one simply does for fun. Play does not seem necessary for survival, and yet humans have a natural desire to play.

The "play" element of sports involves the pleasure of physical movement. Some of the joy we experience from physical play results from moving in ways that we don't typically experience. Practical activities that we all perform every day, such as cleaning or getting dressed, do not give us the physical enjoyment that we get from play. Physical play can create a sense of freedom by allowing us to test our physical limits. We experience a different range of emotions while playing than we do in our everyday life. There is a joy and an excitement to physical play that cannot be felt any other way.[3]

Many sociologists consider play to be an important part of personal and social development. Play can be a way to safely experiment with imaginary situations. It is a type of fantasy that avoids the serious consequences of social reality. As we play, we challenge ourselves in new ways and learn how to cooperate with others. Playing helps us to develop socially by experimenting with different ways of relating to others.

Play is also a form of freedom. When rules are involved, freedom is restricted, but players are still free in ways they are not free in everyday life. Games are organized play, often including rules. Contests, or competitions, are games with a goal—either to beat an opponent or to top a record. Games and competitions are a type of play. We don't do them because we have to, but rather because we want to. People tend to enjoy games more for the activity itself than for the outcome.[4]

"When we were kids there was the release in playing, the sweetness in being able to move and control your body. This is what play is. Beating somebody is secondary."[5]

Eric Nesterenko, National Hockey League player from 1951 to 1972 for the Toronto Maple Leafs and the Chicago Black Hawks

Are modern sports still a form of play? Should play have to follow the same rules and values that apply to society at large? This is something to consider as you read this book.

Palestinian boys in Jerusalem play soccer in the street. Many young people naturally turn to sports for a fun activity.

The work ethic

Despite being a form of play, sports are also related to survival skills. The use of tools and weapons by early humans required practice. Eventually these skills became competitive. When practicing a skill, early humans tested themselves against others to measure their degree of skill.[6] For example, the ability to throw a spear farther than anyone else in a social group became a mark of distinction. (The Olympic sport of javelin throwing is a modern version of such competitions.)

Oleksandr Pyatnytsya of Ukraine throws a javelin during the European Athletics Championships in Barcelona, Spain, in 2010. Javelin throwing is one of the oldest forms of athletic competition to develop from a survival skill.

Spear throwing and other hunting exercises were the dominant forms of early sports for centuries. Such activities were not just essential to survival. They were also a demonstration of physical superiority. This has been a traditional element of sports up to and including modern times. Athletes represent the high degree of skill and strength valued by society.

When play takes on a practical goal, such as learning a survival skill, it becomes a form of work. "Work" is a purposeful activity done to survive or gain social status. Work may sometimes be enjoyable for its own sake and feel like a game. Or it may be the opposite of play—hard work with no sense of satisfaction.

Sports include many worklike elements. For example, serious athletes must work hard at improving their skills by practicing and keeping a strict schedule. At the professional level, sports participation becomes a job or career on which athletes depend to earn a living.

Health and recreation

Beyond play and work, there are other reasons people enjoy the physical activity of sports. Sports can be undertaken as exercise or simply serve as a way to release energy. Physical activity can relieve stress.

Recreation is a type of activity undertaken for the purpose of improving health or physical fitness. Recreation may also involve an enjoyment of the outdoors. Many sports that primarily involve physical activity or a struggle against nature, such as mountain climbing, are typically considered recreational—although organized sports may also be played for recreational reasons.

Foxhunting

Foxhunting is an example of a survival skill that evolved to become a sport. Hunting began as a practical pursuit of animals for food. Common people in the Middle Ages (the 400s to 1400s) enjoyed hunting, seeing it as a contest against nature. For hundreds of years, the hunting of various animals was the main form of sports in England.

Over time, foxes became a standard target of hunters, originally because they pestered farmers. Starting in the 1500s, foxhunting became a tradition among the upper classes. In early forms of foxhunting, people killed the foxes with weapons. Over time, hound dogs were used to track the foxes, with people controlling the hounds. The excitement of the hunt came more from the thrill of the chase than the kill.[7]

Many people do not consider foxhunting a sport today. In response to complaints from groups that saw foxhunting as cruel to animals, England and Wales officially banned hound-assisted foxhunting in 2004.[8]

War preparation

Sports also have their origins in preparations for war. There are many examples of ancient societies in which sports were primarily a method of battle training.

In ancient Greece, sports were a form of training for the warrior class. The popular Greek sport *pankration* combined elements of boxing and wrestling, much like "ultimate fighting" today. But despite their violent nature, Greek sports also focused on athletics.

The warrior-athletes of Sparta

Of all the warring city-states of ancient Greece, Sparta was the most obsessed with military training. Boys of the wealthy warrior class started training at age seven and began military duty at age twenty. Because of their disciplined social order and intense devotion to military drill practice, Spartans dominated athletics in Greece. Constant military training enabled Spartan athletes to stay in peak physical condition. Between 720 and 576 BCE, Spartans won 56 of 71 known Olympic contests against athletes from other city-states. For Spartans, the Olympics were an opportunity to demonstrate their athletic superiority, while also showing off their military strength.[9]

In the 5th century BCE, Persian kings developed what became the modern sport of polo as battle training for the best cavalry units (groups of soldiers who fought on horseback). In polo, teams of riders on horseback race at high speeds to hit a wooden ball into a goal with a mallet. The training, which involved playing games much like miniature battles, was meant to train the horses as much as the riders.[10]

Ancient Roman sports were entirely pursued as combat, with no interest in athletics for their own sake. One of the most popular events was a fight to the death between armed gladiators. Battles were waged for entertainment. The social attitude toward death and suffering in Roman society did not place much value on human life.[11]

In the Middle Ages in Europe, knights engaged in tournaments that resembled actual battles. Sometimes these tournaments were just as deadly—or more so—than actual battles.[12] Among the common people, popular ball games also resembled battles between towns or families.

Polo, one of the earliest team sports, has become an upper-class sport in modern times, although it was once mainly a method of preparing cavalry units for war.

However, there have also been times when sports were seen as a break from the seriousness of war. During important historical moments, sports have been accused of distracting from war preparations. For example, authorities attempted to prohibit ball games as early as 1314, because they considered them a distraction from the more important task of training archers to defend the kingdom.[13]

The war element of sports still exists today in the form of "battle" between two teams or the struggle for domination between two opposing forces. During the cold war, a period of political tension between the United States and the Soviet Union that lasted from 1947 to 1991, the two countries often clashed through Olympic athletic competitions. The warlike nature of sports is also evident in the way action on the field is described. For example, plays in team sports are sometimes referred to as "attacks," "blitzes," or "surgical strikes."[14]

THE GROWTH OF MODERN SPORTS

Before the 1700s, sports as we know them today did not exist. Ancient societies had sportlike games and competitions, but they were often part of military training, religious rituals, or traditional celebrations. Usually there were no formal rules, no consideration of fairness, and no record keeping. Pre-modern sports were also generally quite violent, as was society in general.

During the Middle Ages, various ball games (see box below) were governed by local customs that were passed down traditionally over centuries. Many aspects of these games were unrestricted, such as the number of people permitted to play (sometimes more than 1,000). There were no referees. Instead, disputes were often settled by fistfights. The ball was kicked, carried, hit with sticks, or even transported by players on horseback. The playing field could vary from miles of open country to the streets of towns. Everyone could play, although games frequently resulted in serious injuries.[1]

Variations of modern football

Football, or "field ball," was once the general name for a wide variety of games that involved carrying, hitting, or kicking a ball across a field. Many different variations of football existed in different places. With the development of written rules in the 1800s, modern versions of football took shape and became the variations we know today.[2]

Sport	First rules	Ball	Players per side	Handling	Physical contact	Field	Goal
Association football (soccer)	1843	Round	5 to 11	Goalkeeper limited	Limited	Rectangle	Posts with crossbar and net
Rugby (Union)	1870	Oval	15	Yes	Yes	Rectangle	Try zone, crossbar with posts
American football	1873	Oval	11	Yes	Yes	Rectangle	End zone, crossbar with posts
Australian rules football	1858	Oval	18	Limited	Yes	Ellipsis	Four posts
Gaelic football (Caid)	1884	Round	15	Limited	Limited	Rectangle	H with net

Societies became more **civilized** as the power of royalty declined. This led to government based on representatives of the upper classes. As fairer systems of law began to appear, the nature of sports also changed. Sports grew less violent as the public's tolerance for violence shrank. Beginning in the 1800s, activities that involved killing animals, such as bullfighting, were no longer considered sports in most cultures. Sports also began to require more self-control from players. As social order increased, people were expected to follow rules and control selfish impulses for the good of all.[3]

Fair play

The idea of **fair play** means that play is safer and more enjoyable when there are agreed rules about what is allowed. Fair play is an important ethical aspect of human social life. As the value and importance of fairness grew, societies came to understand that everyone benefits from agreeing about what is right and wrong. The development of fair play reflected an important stage in the development of human **civilization**.

Fair play in sports resulted in the establishment of rules. These rules reduced the violence and also made competition more balanced—for example, by limiting the number of people on each team. Evidence of fair play in sports can be traced to the early development of rules during the 1500s, although ideas about fairness likely existed much earlier. These developments also made sports more interesting to spectators, because a greater balance of skill resulted in longer games and a higher degree of drama.[4]

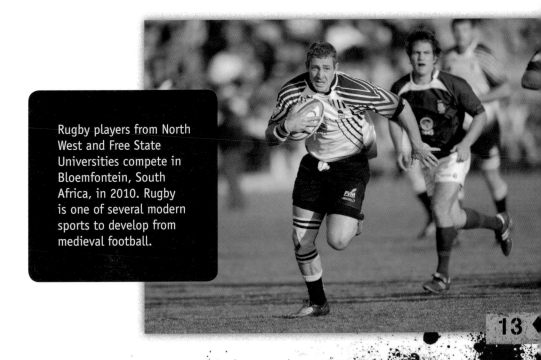

Rugby players from North West and Free State Universities compete in Bloemfontein, South Africa, in 2010. Rugby is one of several modern sports to develop from medieval football.

Rules

Modern sports started in Britain in the 1700s, when many of the first written rules were recorded. Sports played by the upper classes, such as golf and **cricket**, were among the first to become established. The upper classes had more free time than others, and therefore more time to develop their sports. Other sports would become better known as the middle classes gained more political and economic power in the 1800s.[5]

Most sports sociologists consider rules to be the first major characteristic of modern sports. Rules were officially agreed to and written down. This was done to avoid arguments over regional differences in how a game was played. A single set of rules allowed teams and players from different areas to compete in a common form of the game. Rules changed and improved over time, making games fairer and more challenging. The rules of many sports continue to develop even today.

As sports cultures grew and rules became established, this led to the creation of **leagues** and other organizations. A league is a group of sports teams organized to compete against one another. Rules and leagues are generally controlled by an organization that directs the development of a sport. These innovations in sports culture make up what we now know as modern sports.

Records

Modern sports are also defined by several other characteristics, such as achievement and record breaking. Records and statistics are a measure of value in sports. Today, scores are even awarded to sports that do not involve making goals, such as gymnastics. Individuals score points given out by a panel of judges who rate the quality of the performance.

Records serve as a scale to evaluate performance over time. Athletes not only compete with one another, but also with everyone who has ever competed in that sport. This aspect of sports culture is a reflection of modern culture, which favors measurable progress and winning. In this way, sports confirm the cultural values of modern society.[6]

"The faint line of the finishing tape stood ahead as a haven of peace, after the struggle. The arms of the world were waiting to receive me if only I reached the tape without slackening my speed. If I faltered, there would be no arms to hold me and the world would be a cold, forbidding place, because I had been so close. I leapt at the tape like a man taking his last spring to save himself from the chasm that threatens to engulf him."[7]

Runner Roger Bannister, describing the moment when he broke a world record on May 6, 1954, to become the first person to run a mile in under four minutes (3:59.4)

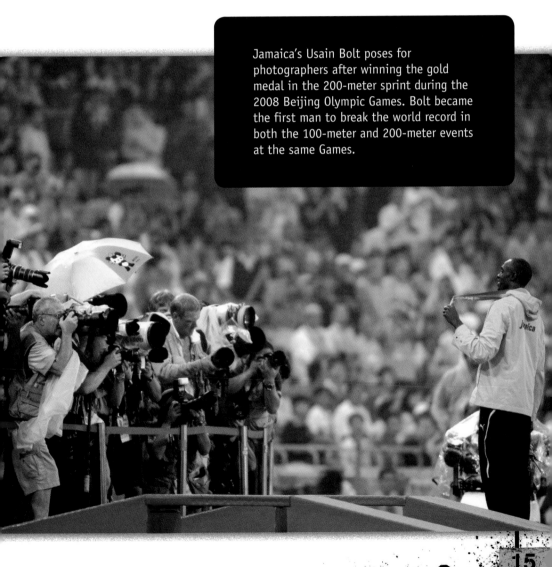

Jamaica's Usain Bolt poses for photographers after winning the gold medal in the 200-meter sprint during the 2008 Beijing Olympic Games. Bolt became the first man to break the world record in both the 100-meter and 200-meter events at the same Games.

World sports cultures

Some of the earliest modern sports cultures developed as a result of **industrialization**. This was a change brought to different societies as new technologies were developed. The Industrial Revolution that began in the late 1700s greatly changed Britain and gradually spread to Europe and the United States. Their economies became based on manufacturing, or making things (especially in factories).

The kind of work available in industrialized societies, such as factory work or machine operation, was often boring and repetitive. Industrialized work created a sharper distinction between work time and "free time," or **leisure**, for the middle classes. People turned to sports for a high-energy release from boredom.[8]

Industrialized societies also had modern school systems, which provided sports training and playing fields for students. Modern sports culture directly resulted from the popularity of sports in British schools and universities at the end of the 1800s. As more young men began to seriously compete in sports, athletics became an important element of social status. Games also began to attract more spectators and to spread to other countries.[9]

Globalization

Sports were introduced to different parts of the world through **globalization**, the spread of economic and cultural connections between nations. Britain's expansion into other lands between 1500 and 1900 brought British culture, including sports such as cricket and rugby, to many countries. In some cases, sports were forced on native cultures, as Britain tried to pass on its cultural values.

In India, Australia, and the islands of the Caribbean, local people originally adopted cricket to reflect the culture of Britain. But, over time, the sport eventually took on a different purpose. It became a way for native teams to assert their own cultural identity and athletic skill in competition against British teams.[10]

In the Dominican Republic, a country in the Caribbean, baseball has also taken on a life of its own. Although Dominican players are often recruited to play in U.S. leagues, Dominican baseball has its own distinct style. For many Dominicans, it is a cheap, peaceful pastime that fills the months between harvests. Each form of baseball is particular to the culture that plays it.[11]

Cricket spread to India through the cultural influence of the British Empire. Sports can take root in new cultures as a form of competition against the culture that imports the sport.

Baseball in Japan

The variations in U.S. and Japanese baseball (known as *yakyu*, or "field ball") reveal important differences between the two cultures. Pacific League *yakyu* games are allowed to end in a tie, whereas U.S. games continue into extra innings until ties are broken. Most Japanese *yakyu* teams are named after companies that own them, not cities (as is the case in the United States). *Yakyu* also places stronger emphasis on collective goals and the unity of the team. Individual players are considered less important than the team in *yakyu*.[12]

Cities and sports

The growth of modern sports is closely related to the growth of cities. Modern sports have followed the patterns of **urbanization**, the movement of populations from rural (country) areas to urban (city) areas. Even before modern cities existed, town centers were the main social gathering places. In the modern world of globalized sports cultures, cities serve the same purpose.

City life is restrictive in many ways. More people live within a small space. Open areas of land are scarce. Sports are a way to relieve the tensions and anxieties that are created by living in cities. For both participants and spectators, sports offer relief from the kind of routine and inactive work associated with city life. They also provide a shared social experience. This is especially important in cities, where people tend to feel separate from the people around them.[13]

Soccer's World Cup and the Olympics are two major events that draw the world's attention. These events would not be possible without cities, which include large sports arenas and resources for tourism such as hotels and public transportation. At the same time, an international sporting event can have unintended consequences to a city that hosts it. For example, the city of Atlanta, Georgia, raised $5 billion from hosting the 1996 Olympic Games, which many citizens expected to be spent on revitalizing the city. However, most of this money benefited private institutions, leaving the city to cover the cost of long-term infrastructure improvements.[14]

CIVIC BOOSTERISM

Sports are an important tool for **civic boosterism**. This is the promotion of a town or city in order to raise its status or attract business—and the jobs that go along with both. Sports can attract many good things for a community. A successful team can bring glory to a small town, or a new stadium can declare a city ready for the world's attention. But civic boosterism can sometimes have negative ethical effects for a community when it ignores or minimizes social problems. For instance, cities sometimes spend public funds to subsidize a sports team or build a stadium to generate tourism, when these funds could also be devoted to addressing needs in the community.

Stadiums

Sports stadiums are a major feature of many city skylines. Beyond the architecture and the playing field itself, stadiums are social spaces that transport players and spectators to a different world. They allow people to separate the world of sports from the social reality outside.

Many sports stadiums, such as Maracana Soccer Stadium in Rio de Janeiro, Brazil, are recognizable features of city skylines.

Stadiums can also be valuable community centers, because of their ability to shelter large numbers of people. During Hurricane Katrina in 2005, people driven from their homes by the storm took refuge in the Louisiana Superdome in New Orleans, home of the National Football League (NFL) team the New Orleans Saints. The stadium sheltered 25,000–30,000 people and became a major center of federal rescue operations—although the rescue itself had management problems.[15]

Stadiums can also become **white elephants**, a term that describes expensive, high-maintenance facilities that cannot be removed. When countries host the Olympics or soccer World Cup, they often have to develop or build stadiums to hold the large audience for these events. After the event is over, the stadiums remain. Host cities must then continue to find large-scale events to keep the stadiums in use, in order to justify their expense and upkeep.[16]

Soccer: The people's sport

Soccer is the world's most popular sport, but why? One reason is that games similar to modern soccer were already played by different cultures in various parts of the world as early as 200 BC. Chinese *tsu chu*, French *la soule*, Italian *gioco del calcio*, and the ball games of Britain in the Middle Ages were all similar to modern soccer.[17]

England is credited with the creation of modern soccer. In 1843 students at the exclusive Eton School developed the rules of "football," a generic ball game that varied from place to place. They did so to distinguish it from the version of the game popularized by the Rugby School, which permitted handling the ball. The Eton rules required a higher degree of skill and self-control, as players could only control the ball with their feet and were not allowed to interfere with other players by tackling them. The National Football Association was formed in 1863 to standardize the rules. This allowed different schools to play against one another. The hands-free version of the game came to be known as "soccer," as a slang abbreviation of the "Association" form of the game.[18]

Soccer star Cristiano Ronaldo of Real Madrid in action against AC Milan in Madrid, Spain, in 2010. Many soccer stars are international celebrities because of the worldwide popularity of the sport.

What are the qualities that make soccer appealing to so many different cultures? First of all, soccer is easy to play. The rules are quickly understood, and the only "equipment" needed are a ball and a flat area with defined boundaries. Soccer takes real skill to play at the professional level, but it can also be enjoyed by unskilled players. Many children play soccer, since all it really requires is the ability to run and kick.

Soccer is also a fast game with constant action. It is a near-perfect example of a quality that is highly valued by many modern cultures: the balance between control and chaos. Players are bound by the rules of the game, which prevent them from handling the ball. Otherwise, they are free to perform to the limits of their natural ability.

Modern soccer and specialization

But soccer has also developed some problems due to its popularity. Over the years it has undergone excessive **specialization**, meaning that players have developed particular skills for their specific positions. Players have become extremely effective at limiting the actions of the opposing team. Defensive players tend to be bigger and stronger. Because of this, games tend to be based more on power than skill. Although specialization affects all professional sports, in soccer it has had the effect of significantly lower scoring. Lower scoring means that there is less reward for the tension of the game, which can feel unsatisfying to some viewers.[19]

"Professional soccer, ever more rapid, ever less beautiful, has tended to become a game of speed and strength, fueled by the fear of losing. . . . To win without magic, without surprise or beauty, isn't that worse than losing? In 1994, during the Spanish championship, Real Madrid was defeated by Sporting from Gijón. But the men of Real Madrid played with *enthusiasm*, a word that originally meant 'having the gods within.' The coach, Jorge Valdano, beamed at the players in the dressing room: 'When you play like that,' he told them, 'it's okay to lose.'"[20]

Journalist Eduardo Galeano

Soccer in the United States

Why is it that soccer has not developed an audience in the United States to the same degree that it has in the rest of the world? Low scoring may be one factor. Another explanation may be that the U.S. sports culture has not embraced soccer *because* it is so popular in other countries. The most popular sports in the United States are uniquely American sports such as football, baseball, and basketball. These sports are linked to a sense of national identity, which in itself makes these sports appealing to Americans. But while it is not very popular with U.S. spectators, soccer is one of the most common participation sports for young people in the United States.[21] It is also a popular women's sport. Women players from other countries have moved in order to be able to play professionally in the United States. The Women's Professional Soccer League was set up in 2009, and five international players—among others—came to play in the new league.

Changing traditions

While some sports appeal to many different cultures, others are firmly rooted in specific cultures. Sports that are too closely tied to cultural traditions may have difficulty keeping pace with changing values. For example, professional sumo wrestling has existed in Japan since at least the 1600s, but some parts of sumo wrestling are no longer embraced by the Japanese people.

The Japanese sport of sumo wrestling has kept many of its traditions despite changes in the culture at large.

Many modern sumo fans no longer recognize the value of certain customs, such as violent hazing rituals. (Hazing is when newcomers are forced to perform humiliating and sometimes dangerous tasks.) But sumo officials refuse to alter the sport's traditional elements, insisting that sumo wrestling's value lies in its cultural tradition.[22]

Sumo wrestling has also been hurt by recent evidence of match-fixing. Opponents have been caught communicating about details of a match beforehand. This has added to the perception that sumo wrestling is more of a performance art than a sport. Sumo wrestling has become increasingly unpopular over the years, attracting fewer participants and smaller audiences due to changing cultural perceptions.

Demonstration sports

For many sports, the real proof of their importance is in being recognized by the international community. Until 1992 the Olympics occasionally hosted "demonstration sports," which were sports not considered official Olympic events which were promoted by the host country. Many of these, including surf life-saving (Paris, 1900) and waterskiing (Munich, 1972), were already considered sports in the host country, but they were not recognized as such by the international community. Some, such as basketball and curling, would become official Olympic sports. But demonstration sports were eventually discontinued. This makes it difficult for any new sports to gain international exposure through the Olympics today.[23]

SPORTS OR RECREATION?

Activities such as surfing and running may be considered recreational activities in popular opinion, even though participants consider them sports. How do recreational activities become sports? One key feature that separates recreational competition from sports is an official organizing structure that promotes them. When activities that exist for recreational enjoyment become competitive, organizations form to regulate rules, keep official records, and organize championship events. These organizations can direct the spread of the sport and also provide training.

PLAYING SPORTS

People play sports for a variety of reasons. As we have seen, these reasons may include recreation or the joy of physical movement. Sports also offer the excitement of a challenge, the satisfaction of accomplishment, and recognition from fellow athletes and spectators. Some athletes feel a sense of self-worth from competing and testing themselves against others. The friendships that form between players or with coaches or trainers are also important to many athletes.[1]

But beyond personal motivations, there is a social value to sports participation. Sports help define and shape social behaviors, a process known as **socialization**. Modern sports require athletes to demonstrate socially responsible values, such as fair play. Athletes must also submit to a structure of rules and follow the direction of authorities who regulate behavior, such as coaches, referees, or other administrators. The behaviors learned through sports reinforce the ways people interact in society.

Soccer players arguing with referees has become a common sight. Authorities in sports, such as referees and umpires, help enforce rules and standards of fair play.

Perhaps the most important social value promoted by sports participation is self-control, the ability to control one's behavior. By following a system of rules, players restrain themselves so that everyone in the game may benefit. Self-control is an especially important social quality. Without it, people would be ruled by selfish desires. Although bad behavior, such as tantrums or angry outbursts, is not unknown among professional athletes, such behavior is generally not considered "sportsmanlike." Athletes cannot compete successfully without at least some level of self-control.[2]

Breaking the rules

When athletes break the rules, sociologists view their behavior in several ways. Ordinary rules violations within the game, which lead to penalties, are a common occurrence in most sports and of little ethical concern. But actions with more negative consequences—such as cheating, gambling, or causing deliberate injury to competitors—are considered **unethical**. This is true not just in sports, but also in a larger social context.

Sociologists also recognize a form of breaking the rules that enables players to gain a positive advantage in game play. **Positive deviance** includes actions that allow athletes to become more competitive or perform at a higher level, such as playing despite an injury or taking performance-enhancing drugs. How do you think different ways of breaking the rules in sports undermine social values?[3]

Another example of socialization in sports is cooperation. Members of a team must help each other perform to the best of their individual abilities. Cooperation can even exist among competitors. In bicycle racing, for example, cyclists assist one another by drafting, or riding in front of other riders to block wind resistance. This allows cyclists to conserve energy. Cyclists recognize the value of helping others so that they can be helped as well.[4]

Sports participation can also help people deal with frustration. A society that values winning and achievement can lead to failure and disappointment. Athletes learn that losing is not the end of the world, despite the intense pressure put on players to succeed. Coping with defeat is as much a part of life as celebrating victory, and sports offer experience in both.

Educators and social workers recognize the socializing value of sports participation, which is why sports are so often incorporated into schools and **rehabilitation** programs. But because sports participation is seen as a positive force for young people, the potential negative affects, such as pressure and anxiety, are sometimes ignored.[5]

Identity issues

Modern sports are defined by the ideal of **equality**, which is the idea that anyone can play, regardless of who they are or what their background is. However, there are many barriers to sports participation that arise from social status and identity.[6]

Class

Sports culture traditionally reflects the class structures of society. Wealthy people generally have better access to sports participation. This is because, in any sport, competing at a high level takes time to train and practice—which requires freedom from having to earn a living. Money is also needed to buy equipment, get access to training facilities, and to pay coaches. For many people, social class and economic background can limit the amount of time they can spend participating in sports.

Certain sports are associated with an amount of leisure time available only to people with a certain level of financial freedom. For example, golf not only requires an investment in expensive equipment such as clubs, but also access to golf courses. Golf courses typically exist only in exclusive social centers such as country clubs.[7]

In 1899 the scholar Thorstein Veblen described upper-class sports as "conspicuous leisure." This means that wealthy people find ways to display their wealth and advertise their superior social status. Because the lower classes are defined by their need to work for a living, the upper class avoids activities that seem too much like labor. Instead, people choose pastimes that appear purposeful and reveal a level of skill that can only be achieved during leisure time. In this way, certain sports are associated with different classes, and they can separate one class from another.[8]

Elite sports occasionally become **democratized**, or accessible to various classes. A good example of this is tennis, a sport that limits participation to those with access to tennis courts. Tennis was originally played on grass croquet courts, which only the very wealthy owned because they required constant maintenance. Tennis was linked with the upper classes for many years, but it attracted a wider range of people when public tennis courts could be cheaply constructed from asphalt. Tennis now attracts a wider range of competitors.[9]

Rafael Nadal played against Tomas Berdych in the 2010 Men's Singles Final at Wimbledon.

Technology in sports

Most sports depend on some form of technology, whether a playing field, a kind of ball, or a running shoe. Many modern sports would not be possible without the stopwatch, and referees frequently rely on electronic line judges to determine whether a ball has gone out of bounds.

But some sports lean more heavily on technology than others. This raises questions about whether or not they are sports at all. In auto racing, for example, is the contest between the racers, between the driver and the car, or between the mechanics who maintain the cars? Sports such as yachting, which rely on expensive technology, limit their accessibility to those who can afford them. To what degree is technology necessary for sports?[10]

Gender

Men have traditionally dominated sports. Sports culture in general takes on an aggressively male, or **macho**, tone. Macho ideas of sports emphasize **stereotypically masculine** physical characteristics, such as strength and aggression. As a result, women's participation in sports has often been considered less important than men's.[11]

The macho idea of **gender** roles has limited women's opportunities to participate in sports. The history of female involvement in the Olympics illustrates many of the problems women face. When the modern Olympics began in 1896, women were not allowed to compete, reflecting founder Pierre de Coubertin's opinion that "the Olympic games must be reserved for the solemn and periodic exaltation of male athleticism with . . . female applause as reward."[12]

Women then organized their own athletic events, putting pressure on the International Olympic Committee (IOC) to begin including female events. By 1980 women made up 20 percent of Summer Olympic competitors, which increased to 42 percent by the 2008 Summer Olympics.[13]

Victoria Pendleton was just one of the cyclists who complained about the gender imbalance in track cycling at the 2008 Olympics. There were more men's races than women's races, which meant the women had fewer opportunities to win medals. This imbalance has been resolved for the 2012 Olympics.

In 1991 the IOC ruled that new events must include women. However, women still have to fight to compete in some sports. For example, women's ski jumping was barred from the 2010 Winter Olympics because of vague concerns over the danger. This sparked a lawsuit, which pushed the IOC to include the sport for women in the 2014 Winter Olympics in Russia.[14]

The question of whether to fight to be included in male sporting events or to support all-female events also raises issues of equality. Women's sports are generally underappreciated, receiving fewer resources and less **media** coverage than male events. Tennis is a notable exception, in which the men's and women's events run at the same time and rival one another in popularity. But in general, sports culture maintains the idea that men are better suited to sports and that women's sports are therefore not as important.[15] Perceptions about the role of women in sports can also have a larger impact on how people view women, such as what kinds of jobs women are suited for.

Homophobia

The macho viewpoint of sports affects cultural ideas of sexuality as well as gender. **Homophobia**, the fear and dislike of homosexuality, is especially strong in sports. This is again connected to cultural attitudes about masculinity. Because sports are perceived as a macho area, heterosexuality is assumed among male athletes. In fact, among men, homosexuality is often associated with being bad at sports. Sociologists have found that homosexual athletes face a level of prejudice in sports that often prevents them from publicly revealing their sexuality.[16] In contrast, women may face the opposite assumption—that their involvement in sports is evidence of homosexuality.

Caster Semenya

In August 2009, 18-year-old Caster Semenya of South Africa became world champion of the women's 800-meter race at the world track and field championships in Berlin, Germany. Because of her muscular body and husky voice, competitors suspected her of having male sexual characteristics.

Gender is not always clearly defined as either male or female. Track and field's governing body, the International Association of Athletic Federations, tested Semenya in 2010 to determine her gender. Although the tests confirmed her eligibility to compete as a woman, the controversy raised many questions about the fairness of sexual equality in sports. For people whose gender is not distinctly male or female, the right to compete is a complicated issue.[17]

Race

Race is another part of social identity that affects sports participation. Members of ethnic groups that are in the minority in a society—for example, nonwhite races in the United States—are often **discriminated** against in society and face fewer opportunities for social advancement. **Racism** is the judgment of other races based on prejudice. It may involve physical abuse or name calling, among other things. Sports culture reflects existing racial divisions in society. It can also reinforce or challenge cultural prejudices.[18]

In the United States, African Americans had to play in their own sports leagues for much of the early 1900s. In 1947 Jackie Robinson broke the race barrier in Major League Baseball by joining the Brooklyn Dodgers. This helped pave the way for sports—and society at large—to accept the idea of African Americans becoming an equal part of society. African Americans gradually found more opportunities in sports, as society's views on race changed over time. Now African-American men make up a significant proportion of many sports teams, and many have become major celebrities.[19]

U.S. sprinters Tommie Smith and John Carlos give the Black Power Salute to protest against racism at the 1968 Olympic Games in Mexico City. Race is sometimes ignored as a powerful element in professional sports.

While instances of obvious racism have generally decreased in professional sports, they have not been wiped out completely. Coaches sometimes give players certain positions according to race or ethnicity, a method known as **stacking**. Stacking is based on a pattern of specialization that assumes some ethnicities are more suited to certain positions than others. For example, African Americans typically play defensive and offensive backfield positions in football. Although there are many famous players who break this trend, stacking persists in many sports, and is based on cultural assumptions about race and athletic ability.[20]

Aborigines, the native peoples of Australia, also face many racial barriers to participation in Australian sports. When Aboriginal players are able to compete with white players, they face an intense level of racism. Incidents of racist harassment in Australian football were so common that in 1995 the Australian Football League Commission put rules in place banning racial insults.[21]

Sports culture can overcome racial differences, such as when players of different races cooperate on a team, or when fans identify with a star athlete of a different race. However, sports can also exaggerate racial tensions. Racism can become more of a factor for athletes and spectators in certain situations, for example when boxers of different races fight. The racial divide in sports culture can also take the form of limited opportunities for minorities in management positions, or underrepresentation in sports such as golf.

NATIVE-AMERICAN STEREOTYPES

U.S. sports use elements of Native-American culture in the form of team names, symbols, and mascots. Among many examples are the Atlanta Braves (baseball), the Washington Redskins (football), and the Chicago Blackhawks (hockey). The Florida State University Seminoles claim to have originated the "tomahawk chop," a chopping arm gesture accompanied by a "war chant," meant to reflect stereotypical ideas of warlike native tribes. Many Native Americans object to the use of their culture in this way. They believe it shows a lack of respect for their culture and shows them as violent warriors, which is not the case.[22]

Disability

There are many kinds of disability that can affect athletes, and disability in sports can be a complicated issue. A disability can affect any part of the body or senses. Sometimes it may require technology or human assistance to allow an athlete to participate in sports. Some athletes are born with their disabilities, while others may develop them later in life or become injured. Sports can also be a way to cope and learn to live with a disability. There are many examples of athletes whose disabilities have not affected their ability to compete in mainstream sports. For example, over the years, Major League Baseball has had two one-armed pitchers.[23]

Although some disabled athletes find ways to compete in established sports, some sports have developed to accommodate physical limitations. For instance, wheelchair rugby, also known as quad rugby or murderball, has been played by disabled athletes since 1977. It incorporates wheelchairs into a high-contact form of rugby on an indoor court.[24] To be able to play, individuals must have a disability that affects their arms and legs. They must also be able to move a manual wheelchair with their arms.

Championship sporting events for people with disabilities often run at the same time as, but separate from, mainstream sports events. This wheelchair rugby match took place during the 2008 Paralympic Games in Beijing, China.

Competitions for disabled athletes generally occur separately from other national competitions. The Paralympics, which began in 1960 and include events for a variety of disabilities, run at the same time as the Olympics. Some disabled athletes also compete at the Olympic level. South African swimmer Natalie Du Toit, whose left leg was amputated below the knee, became the first disabled athlete to qualify for an Olympic final in the 2008 Beijing Games.[25]

Identity and exclusion

Although sports culture reflects many existing social prejudices, it also maintains ideas that rank certain kinds of people over others, based on assumptions about their athletic ability. Sports have the power to shape our society—in both positive and negative ways.

Natalie Du Toit was a talented swimmer before a car accident resulted in the loss of her leg. Now she is famous for competing against able-bodied swimmers as well as in the Paralympics.

ATHLETES AND AGING

Many sports have an age range considered best for competition, especially at the professional level. Athletes are often limited by beliefs about how aging limits their ability to participate in sports. However, modern science has helped many athletes perform better than people the same age had in the past. A study found that swimmers between the ages 25 and 55 are faster now than that same age group was 20 years ago. Better nutrition, advances in sports medicine, and improved training techniques are allowing athletes to participate in sports later into their lives than ever before.[26]

Regionalism and rivalry

Many professional sports teams are associated with particular cities or regions, which adds another level of identity to sports participation. Local teams represent a sense of community that players and fans share. Sometimes the strength of regional loyalty has little to do with the success of the team. Instead, it is related to local pride and the ways people associate their social identity with supporting a team.

Fierce loyalty to local teams and rivalry toward other teams can create a greater sense of community and belonging. But it can also exaggerate the division between otherwise similar sports cultures. Even within a single city, loyalties can be divided. For example, U.S. baseball fans in New York are divided between the Mets and the Yankees, and soccer fans in Manchester, England, are divided between Manchester City and Manchester United.[27]

German soccer fans wave flags during the 2008 Euro semifinal between Germany and Turkey in Berlin. Patriotism is often closely tied to team loyalty.

Supporting local teams can lead to heated competitions between teams or players. One of the biggest rivalries in soccer is between Real Madrid and Barcelona. The two teams not only represent Spain's two largest cities, but they also have different cultural and political associations. Barcelona is closely identified with the Catalan culture of northeastern Spain. When the two teams play each other, the match is known as *El Clásico* ("The Classic"), and it is one of the most-watched games in soccer.[28]

Many of the longest-running rivalries go beyond sports to express general feelings of pride. For example, Harvard and Yale are academic rivals, but they also compete in football and crew (rowing).[29]

Not all rivalries are related to negative feelings. Rivalries can sometimes be friendly, as with the tennis rivalry between Roger Federer and Rafael Nadal.[30]

Rivalries add to the drama of sports, but they can also have negative real-world consequences when fans take them too seriously. This is especially true when teams are invested with feelings of national pride. In 1969 the bad feelings created by a qualifying round of games between Honduras and El Salvador for the 1970 soccer World Cup led to a four-day military confrontation known as the Soccer War.[31]

"On the village green, where you pick up sides and no feeling of local **patriotism** is involved, it is possible to play simply for the fun and exercise: but as soon as the question of **prestige** arises, as soon as you feel that you and some larger unit will be disgraced if you lose, the most savage combative instincts are aroused. . . . But the significant thing is not the behavior of the players but the attitude of the spectators: and, behind the spectators, of the nations who work themselves into furies over these absurd contests, and seriously believe—at any rate for short periods—that running, jumping and kicking a ball are tests of national virtue [goodness]."[32]

Author George Orwell, "The Sporting Spirit" (1945)

Nationalism

Organized sports are also subject to **nationalism**, the identification with one's country. On the plus side, patriotic feelings can inspire athletes. The downside to such thinking, however, is that members of competing nations may view each other in a negative light.

Nationalist tendencies in sports are at their most obvious during international competitions, when athletes or teams represent their home countries. Ever since the modern Olympics began in 1896, the competitions have been a showcase not just for athletic talent and skill, but also for representations of national pride.[33]

The most dramatic example of the government use of sports to promote nationalist goals is the 1936 Olympics held in Nazi Germany. The Nazi Party believed in the superiority of Germans and German culture. This idea contributed to the deaths of more than 6 million Jews by the end of World War II in 1945, when the Nazi Party was removed from power.

Nazi banners decorate the lighting of the Olympic flame in Berlin during the opening ceremonies of the 1936 Olympic Games. The 1936 Games are often associated with the Nazis' displays of nationalism.

In 1936 sports in Germany had become a patriotic activity. Athletes were closely associated with national strength and pride. The Nazis were also fascinated with mass festivals and displays of power, of which the Olympics is one of the biggest in the world. The Nazis were determined to overshadow previous Olympics. This tradition continues to this day, with each new Olympics designed to be more impressive than the last. [34]

Ping-pong diplomacy

In the 1970s tensions were high between the governments of the United States and China. The two countries had fought during the Korean War (1950–53), and they had not had diplomatic relations since the Communist Party founded the People's Republic of China in 1949. The thaw in relations finally came through a series of ping-pong games between the two national teams in the early 1970s. This helped improve relations. It demonstrated the positive role that athletes can have in relations between nations. Athletic competitions can test whether countries are able to get along and pave the way to greater cultural understanding. [35]

South Africa

Sports as a nationalist tool can also be seen in South Africa. Starting in the 1950s, South Africa had been the focus of a worldwide economic and sports boycott (refusal to trade or participate in international sporting events) because of its policy of apartheid, which separated black and white people.

Apartheid ended in 1994 when Nelson Mandela and the African National Congress came to power. In 1995 South Africa hosted and won the Rugby World Cup, an event that united blacks and whites in support of the national team, the Springboks. This is a positive example of how sports can bring people together in national pride. [36]

However, many of the economic **inequalities** that existed during apartheid remain or have gotten worse. The government of South Africa hosted the soccer World Cup in 2010 and hoped to improve the country's image. In order to do this, it built stadiums out of sight of the poor conditions in which many of its citizens live. In Mbombela, the building of a new stadium forced many people from their homes. The economic benefits created by big sporting events like the soccer World Cup, such as development and jobs, often don't result in long-term improvements for the people who live in the host country. [37]

WATCHING SPORTS

Modern sporting events are more than just games or competitions. They are also **spectacles**, entertaining displays that impress and attract viewers. Watching sports can provide a variety of pleasures and interest the spectator on many levels.[1]

For spectators, there is the general expectation of excitement and the potential for an impressive accomplishment—like the breaking of a record or a last-minute goal. There is also the satisfaction of witnessing the skillful execution of a difficult maneuver. For example, viewers of the 2009 U.S. Open semifinal tennis match between Roger Federer and Novak Djokovic witnessed an amazing moment toward the end of the match, when Federer returned the ball from behind his back and between his legs. Such moments are an essential part of the thrill of watching sports.[2]

Beyond the game itself, sporting events can make a sports viewer feel part of something significant. Most modern sporting events are designed to heighten this impression, with added entertainment elements to build up and intensify the main event. For example, during pregame press conferences, athletes or managers build up anticipation for the game by demonstrating their confidence or assessing the strength of the opposing team. Such conferences add background to the main event, which increases the entertainment value for spectators.

For especially devoted sports viewers, there are also intellectual pleasures to following sports. Sports coverage indulges an interest in strategies and statistics through live commentaries, television talk shows, and analysis in newspapers and magazines. Spectators can learn details about athletes and trends in the sport, developing an insight into the sport that rewards continued interest.[3]

All of the elements of sports culture, from the game itself to the entertainment surrounding the game, set a game apart from the everyday life of the sports viewer. Sports become a strongly defined world, with their own sense of order and spectacular moments of freedom. This helps make watching sports an escape from everyday reality.

The Super Bowl

Football's championship game, the Super Bowl, is a cultural spectacle unlike any other. Many people who don't follow football watch the Super Bowl because of its status as a major cultural event, which ultimately includes much more than the game itself.

The Super Bowl often lasts up to four hours. Some of this time is entertainment, such as the pregame and halftime shows, which usually involves popular music performances and technical displays. The Super Bowl is also an advertising showcase. Advertising time during the game costs more than at any other time of the year and takes up to 40 minutes of the total broadcast time. Media coverage of the Super Bowl supports the impression that the game is an event of particular social importance—almost a national holiday.[4]

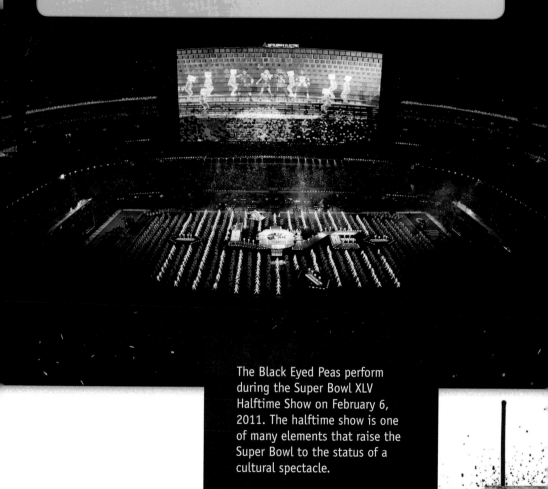

The Black Eyed Peas perform during the Super Bowl XLV Halftime Show on February 6, 2011. The halftime show is one of many elements that raise the Super Bowl to the status of a cultural spectacle.

Religion

Although modern sports may not seem spiritual, religion and sports are historically closely linked. In many ancient societies, sports were an element of religious worship, performed as ceremonies to please the gods in order to assure fertility (the ability to have children), bring successful crops or good weather, cure sickness, or keep demons away. Games were often tied to a sacred place and time of year. Many religious sporting **rites** were also heavily symbolic. Two competing teams might represent a natural balance, as with the Plains Indians of North America, whose teams in an ancient ceremonial ball game symbolized the sun and moon.[5]

Sports became less religious, or more **secular**, over time. They began to be enjoyed for their own sake. This corresponded to similar changes in the rest of society, which also moved toward more secular ways of social organization.

The lighting of the Olympic flame at the 2004 Games in Athens, Greece, reminds us of the ancient religious function of sports.

Forms of religious ceremony survive in the opening ceremony of the Olympic Games. The ancient Olympic Games were a sacred festival to honor the god Zeus. They included many ceremonial rituals like the ones performed today, such as the lighting of the Olympic torch. The meaningful feeling created by these sorts of rituals was closely tied to a sense of community in ancient societies. With their gatherings of large numbers of people, modern sports create a similar sense of participation in something larger than one's self.[6]

There are many similarities between religion and modern sports. Some sociologists have suggested that the sense of community in modern sports meets some of the social needs once fulfilled by religion in society. Sports have been called a "surrogate [substitute] religion," inspiring a devotion and following once claimed by more religious cultures. Like religion, sports have become meaningful for many people, influencing the way people structure their lives and how they define themselves. Sports can inspire strong feelings and create the impression of a connection with something beyond the everyday world.[7]

Sociologist Allen Guttmann associates modern society's focus on achievement in sports, for example through setting records, with an expression of larger cultural values, such as those promoted by the religious nature of sports in ancient societies. According to Guttmann, the value of sports participation as a connection to a sense of living forever through statistical accomplishment is similar to the social function of sports as an ancient religious rite.[8]

SUPERSTITION IN SPORTS

Many players, coaches, and fans engage in **superstitious** behavior. This is often an attempt to control their fears over the outcome of a game. Such behavior can involve diet (eating, or avoiding, a certain food only on game day), clothing (wearing special clothes), taboos (avoiding anything considered unlucky), the use of "lucky" objects or equipment, or a pregame ritual (an activity performed to bring luck). While not generally considered religious, superstition has its roots in spiritual practices that tried to gain the favor of the gods. Similarly, the superstitious belief that an activity will influence the outcome of a game is an example of the need to feel in control of something that cannot really be controlled.[9]

The art of sports

Performance is an important factor in the entertainment value of sports. Spectators are attracted by the display of skill and the feats of speed and strength that occur during athletic competitions. The **aesthetic** element of sports, meaning the part that is concerned with an appreciation of grace or skill, is sometimes not fully recognized. While all sports have aesthetic elements, some sports provide more aesthetic performances than others.

The appeal of performance-based sports such as gymnastics and figure skating is mostly based on aesthetics. They are judged on the quality of the graceful performance of athletic feats. What separates such sports from performance-based art, such as dance? One way to distinguish sports performance from artistic performance is by the need for an audience. Gymnastics are a performance, but they are also enjoyable for the gymnast if he or she were alone in an empty room. Although the same may be true of dance, artistic performance is more purposeful in its aim to communicate with an audience. Dance and gymnastics may not be so different, but the importance of the audience is different for each of them.[10]

Another element of performance in sports is **grandstanding**, or putting on a show for the audience. Grandstanding typically occurs after a point is scored, when athletes celebrate their victory by dancing or signaling to the crowd. This kind of behavior is generally considered unprofessional by sports administrators, as athletes are not supposed to play to the crowd.

What role does performance play in regular athletic competition? The ultimate point of many athletic activities is to score points or excel above a competitor. However, as we have seen from looking at "play" (see pages 6 and 7), part of the pleasure of a game is the way it is played rather than the end goal. The role of aesthetics in sports is largely a matter of the quality of the experience for spectators. For example, the sight of a top athlete such as Michael Jordan launching through the air to dunk a basketball could be considered more satisfying to spectators than the actual points scored. The beauty of the game—the quality of the skill on display—is part of what makes sports appealing.

Nadia Comaneci's perfect-10 gymnastic performance at the 1976 Montreal Olympics is a strong example of aesthetics in sports.

NADIA COMANECI (1961–)

In the 1976 Summer Olympics in Montreal, Canada, 14-year-old Romanian gymnast Nadia Comaneci became the first Olympic athlete to be awarded a "perfect 10" score. She eventually received six more perfect 10s and earned three gold medals for the uneven bars, balance beam, and all-around competition. Comaneci became an overnight celebrity known the world over as "Nadia." She was featured on the covers of *Time*, *Newsweek*, and *Sports Illustrated*. After returning home, she was a hero in her country.[11]

Media

Like sports, the mass media expanded dramatically during the 1900s. Newspapers, magazines, radio, television, and the Internet influence how we see the world. Today, sports have their own section in most daily newspapers. Television features all-sports cable channels as well as pay-per-view access to games. Major networks compete to show important sports or games, with viewing rights for events such as the Olympics and soccer World Cup costing billions of dollars. Sports are important in the media because they have such a devoted following and a guaranteed audience.[12]

The media and entertainment industries can also be sources of employment opportunities for retired athletes. Because their experience gives them a valuable inside perspective, former players are often recruited as commentators, play-by-play announcers, or sports analysts. Many retired or active players can also earn money through other media or entertainment-related opportunities, such as by signing autographs or appearing at events or in television shows or movies.

Often the business side of sports causes a media sensation as well. When NBA All-Star LeBron James became a free agent (able to sign a new contract with any team) upon ending his contract with the Cleveland Cavaliers in 2010, he was free to accept the highest salary bids to play for a different team. His attempted recruitment by six teams became a major news story, ending with an hour-long television special to announce James' decision to join the Miami Heat.[13]

Celebrity

Some athletes break beyond the barriers of sports to become celebrities in their own right. Today, soccer star David Beckham is arguably as well known for his celebrity marriage to pop star and fashion designer Victoria Beckham as he is for his skills on the field. In 2007 Beckham and his wife appeared on a one-hour television program that followed the celebrity couple as they found their way in their newly adopted city of Los Angeles.[14]

As athletes are idolized and made into media stars, they are celebrated but also closely examined. Many sports stars are known as much for their behavior off the sports field as on it. In 2010 one of the biggest scandals in sports history broke when numerous women reported that they had had affairs with professional golfer Tiger Woods. Woods, married with two children, had been seen as a role model for much of his career. After the scandal became an international news story, Woods' golf career and his celebrity status suffered a major setback.[15]

British Formula 1 race-car driver Lewis Hamilton poses for photographers at the Brazilian Grand Prix 2010 in Sao Paulo, Brazil. Celebrities and media in sports both reinforce each other.

Second chances

In 2007 Atlanta Falcons football player Michael Vick was convicted of operating a dogfighting ring and sentenced to 23 months in prison. Vick's crime, animal torture, is so looked down upon by society that it was doubtful whether he would return to professional football.

Vick was released from prison in 2009, after serving 18 months, and the Philadelphia Eagles hired him. He was given the starting quarterback position and quickly established himself as one of the NFL's most valuable players. Vick's turnaround raises questions about the ethical value of forgiveness in sports culture. Does an impressive athletic performance make people forgive a player for a moral offense?[16]

Commercialization

Huge amounts of money fuel the sports industry, creating a network of jobs and services only loosely related to actual sports. Sports have become a big business. In modern sports, **commercialization**, the process that emphasizes the business or moneymaking side of sports, continues to expand.

For athletes, success in sports is no longer connected to just status or a trophy. Salaries have become quite large in order to attract and keep valuable players. This means that players compete not just to win the game, but also sometimes against players on their own team to be the most valuable—and therefore highest-paid—player.[17] In 2010 basketball star LeBron James was the highest-paid contracted player, earning more than $15.7 million, not including deals to **endorse** products.[18] Tournament winnings can bring in even more money. In 2010 boxer Floyd Mayweather, Jr., earned the highest income from winnings, at $60 million.[19]

The modern sports culture is full of **sponsorships**. Advertisements can be seen on stadium walls, players' uniforms, programs, and commercial breaks during televised pauses in game play. Professional athletes are paid large amounts of money to endorse products. In 2010 golf star Tiger Woods earned $7,737,000 in winnings from tournaments, but he made $92 million in endorsements and advertising—more than any other athlete.[20] (However, Woods was expected to lose millions in endorsements in 2011 following the scandal in his personal life; see page 44.)

THE SUPERSTAR EFFECT

The pay of superstar athletes has increased dramatically over the years. For example, Cristiano Ronaldo, soccer's highest-paid player in 2010, made 15 times as much as Pelé did in 1960, when he was soccer's biggest superstar.[21] Growing salaries for the highest-paid athletes can create a sense of inequality that affects society in general. Studies have shown that pay scales that reward those at the top much more than others can contribute to a feeling of social unfairness and dissatisfaction among those at the low end of the pay scale. These people feel that their efforts are not being properly rewarded.[22]

In many countries, buying merchandise is a major part of sports culture. Many fans consider merchandise to be a badge of loyalty for a team. Shirts, hats, flags, and other memorabilia bearing team logos make up a major market for sports vendors.

Sports merchandise, such as a stand at the 2010 soccer World Cup in South Africa, has become an important element of the sports experience for spectators.

As ticket prices generally continue to rise, people find ways to buy sought-after tickets to resell at significantly higher prices. With the increasing cost of attending sporting events, sports administrators must invest more into the events to make spectators feel that they are getting their money's worth.[23]

The extreme commercialization of sports has met with resistance from some people. Sociologists, and even some athletes, worry that sports are no longer played for the enjoyment of the game if money is a major force behind a sport.

Fans and fantasy

Identity, an important factor in sports participation, is perhaps even more important to spectators. Devoted sports spectators are known as "fans," short for "**fanatics**"—a term that describes a person who shows extreme enthusiasm. The intense passion fans feel results from identifying with certain teams or athletes in ways similar to those that we looked at earlier: **regionalism**, national pride, or some other special identity characteristic of personal value to a fan. Fans may also feel an attachment to a sport that they grew up playing or watching, or perhaps they cherish the sense of community with fellow fans or the rituals that sports cultures provide.

The engaging atmosphere that fans create around sports allows for the expression and acknowledgment of emotions that typically do not get displayed in public. It is rare to find any other areas of society where joy and excitement can be expressed as freely as in the stands of a sporting event.[24]

Sports culture can inspire an active fantasy life for fans. As fans identify with star athletes, they experience the thrill of their triumphs and share in their defeats. Sociologists call this form of identification **BIRGing**, short for "basking in reflected glory." It can have the effect of boosting a spectator's self-esteem simply through witnessing another person's accomplishments. BIRGing is clearly a meaningful experience for many sports spectators. Sports culture offers fans an escape from the cares of the world, highlighted by moments of glory and freedom.[25]

FAN CULTURE

Fans' desires to express their identification with a favorite team or athlete can take different forms. Some fans paint their bodies or faces with team or national colors, wear crazy costumes, or hold up banners with the names of favorite players. Fans may also organize "fantasy leagues," where they pick imaginary teams based on real players and play out an imaginary season based on actual statistics.

Fan devotion can sometimes turn negative as well, such as when fans attempt to interfere with a game by jeering opposing players or throwing things onto the field. All of these activities give fans the impression of active participation in the game, making fans an important element of sports culture.

South Africa supporters show their team pride at a 2010 soccer World Cup match against Mexico in Johannesburg, South Africa. Fans will often go to great lengths to express their identification with their favorite teams.

Gambling

Sports culture is often associated with gambling, or betting money on the outcome or details of a game. Most gambling is done illegally. Betting allows spectators to more closely identify with the competitors by staking something important—their money—on the outcome. The social consequences of gambling are well known. It can become an addiction that results in serious personal consequences. Gambling even affects sports directly, when teams or players are paid to throw a game or shave points.[26]

Violence

As we have seen, sports culture historically becomes less violent when society moves toward more peaceful methods for resolving social and political conflicts (see pages 12 and 13). One example of how sports culture reflects this change in attitudes toward violence can be found in the history of boxing.

In the mid-1700s, bare-fist boxing underwent changes that improved its cultural status. London gym owner Jack Broughton is credited with introducing boxing gloves, known as "mufflers," in the early 1740s, as well as rules and restrictions for hitting below the belt. "Broughton's rules" were created to attract gentlemen to his gym, but they also made the sport safer and more acceptable, allowing boxing to overcome society's lowered tolerance for violent sports. In 1865 the written "Queensberry rules" drafted by J. G. Chambers laid the foundation for modern boxing, limiting the number of rounds and making gloves a requirement.[27]

Safer technology has an ethical downside, however. Boxing gloves were introduced to protect the boxer's face and fists from impact, which enabled matches to last longer and therefore be more entertaining to spectators. But it also made boxing dangerous in other ways. Even though contestants were protected from serious injury, they had to endure more powerful punches over a longer period of time. This resulted in different types of injuries that were less visible to spectators, such as internal bruising or brain damage.[28]

Head injuries in football

Football is a violent game, involving head-on collisions, hard tackles, and broken limbs. Head injuries have been taken for granted since football first became popular in the United States in the 1960s. But the serious nature of head injuries, particularly undiagnosed concussions, became a national issue in the early 2000s, when studies showed that long-term brain damage had developed in many former NFL players. Government hearings on the issue led to stricter NFL policies regarding recovery time for a head injury and closer attention to helmet safety standards. Still, the problem remains unresolved. The issue of football head injuries shows how modern sports continue to strive for increased safety, while at the same time maintaining their violent nature.[29]

But why do violent sports continue to attract spectators? Many popular sports contain a degree of violent contact. Some sociologists consider sports a release valve for violent impulses. This release comes both through watching violence on the field or in the ring, and also through participating in the stands.

Hooliganism

Perhaps the biggest social problem stemming from sports violence is **hooliganism**, or fan violence directed at players, referees, or, most often, opposing fans. In 1964 at least 287 people were killed during a riot at an international soccer match between Peru and Argentina in Lima, Peru. This was one of the worst instances of hooliganism in modern times.[30]

Although it has occurred in various sports as far back as 1870, hooliganism today is often associated with soccer. Sociologist Eric Dunning has traced the hooliganism of some British soccer fans to a larger social pattern of aggressive masculine conflict between the working class and the police in areas where hooliganism primarily occurs. In any case, hooliganism offers a real-world outlet for the violence enjoyed as entertainment on the field.[31]

Violence in sports culture, especially as a form of entertainment, continues to raise serious ethical concerns. Do violent sports merely relieve violent urges? Or do they encourage them?

Liverpool soccer fans begin to riot before kickoff at the 1985 European Cup Final against Juventus in Brussels. In total, 39 people were killed and hundreds more were injured.

THE ETHICS OF SPORTS CULTURE

Sports culture seems to reflect many conflicting aspects of social life. Sports are both work and play, fantasy and reality, games and business. They offer a joyous sense of freedom within an ordered structure of rules. Sports bring people together in a common culture, while at the same time creating divisions based on class, region, race, and gender. Sports can be a force for both good and bad in society.

Thousands of runners take part in marathons and runs for charity each year. Marathons are an example of sports as a social activity.

Sports can have many valuable social benefits. People may play sports for health and fitness, or to enjoy the thrill of testing physical limits. Socialization through sports can help us learn how to reach our potential as individuals, while still looking out for the interests of all. It can also teach us the value of fair play and the structure of rules. Many people, whether as athletes or spectators, find sports a meaningful source of social identity and an important ego-boosting activity. But most of all, sports are fun and exciting entertainment, an escape from everyday life, and a needed release from the stress of social pressures.

But ethical problems can also stem from several features of modern sports culture. One is the ability of sports to emphasize differences and reinforce values that leave out or undervalue certain people based on gender, sexuality, race, class, and ability. If people become too caught up in the fantasy of sports, they also risk minimizing the important issues of reality. The emphasis on achievement and winning in sports can also have the effect of taking away from the pure joy of "play." This leads to cheating, drugs, violence, and greed. And perhaps most importantly, violence both on the field and off has continued to define sports culture, even as society's tolerance for violence has lessened.

How do we balance these different aspects of sports? As sports cultures continue to grow and evolve, the sociological study of sports can be a valuable way to recognize sports' social benefits—while also addressing the ethical problems that can result from fun and games.

What do you think?

In what ways are sports a positive force in society? How do sports negatively affect the way we live? In your personal experience, are sports beneficial? How do sports affect your life, either as a participant or as a spectator?

TOPICS FOR DISCUSSION

As this book has shown, there are many issues surrounding the relationship between sports, culture, and sociology. Here are a few more questions to consider:

- How does your personal experience of sports relate to issues raised in this book?

- Why is it necessary to study sports from the perspective of sociology?

- Is the focus on winning and achievement in modern sports a positive force?

- Is the behavior of professional athletes important to society?

- Do athletes have the responsibility to be good role models?

- Do sports benefit local communities?

- Should political influence be used to promote sports, as in the case of the Olympics hosted by the Nazi Party (see page 36)?

- How much involvement should governments have in sports?

- Are regionalism and nationalism important to sports participation?

- Should public resources, such as tax money or land, be used for sports?

- Should everyone have equal access to sports trainers, facilities, and so on?

- Think about cultural perceptions that result from differences in athletic performance based on gender, race, or disability. How do these perceptions contribute to discrimination in society?

- What social problems result from cultural values that are based on differences in athletic ability?

- Is the commercialization of sports harmful to sports?

- Does the desire to make money take away from sports as entertainment?

- Do athletes deserve to earn enormous salaries?

- Why do violent sports, such as boxing, continue to appeal to some sports fans?

- Who is responsible for social problems that arise from sports culture, such as fan violence?

- How can behaviors that have negative social consequences in sports be changed?

GLOSSARY

aesthetic quality that appeals to a sense of beauty or grace

BIRGing (short for "basking in reflected glory") method by which spectators identify with athletes to experience the thrill of their triumphs

civic boosterism promotion of a town or city in order to raise its status or attract business

civilization human society that has developed advanced forms of cultural, political, and scientific organization

civilized having a high degree of social and cultural development

commercialization process that emphasizes business or moneymaking

cricket game played between two teams of 11 players that is popular in many places around the world, including Britain, Australia, New Zealand, South Asia, the Caribbean, and South Africa

culture shared values and lifestyle characteristics of a society

democratize make society become more equal

discriminate to judge a person according to differences based on race, gender, class, or other social factors

endorse in sports, for a professional athlete to be paid to support or promote a product or service

equality in sports, the idea that anyone can play, regardless of who they are or what their background is

ethical relating to ethics, or issues of right and wrong

ethics study of issues of right and wrong as they relate to human behavior

fair play respectful and honorable interaction that ensures the safety and enjoyment of an athletic competition

fanatic person who shows extreme enthusiasm for something, such as a sports team

gender sexual identity; being male or female

globalization spread of economic and cultural connections between nations

grandstanding performing to impress an audience

homophobia hatred and fear of homosexuality

hooliganism violence begun by sports fans

industrialization social and economic transformation that resulted from the development of new technologies beginning in Britain in the 1700s

inequality unequal balance of social relationships; injustice

league group of sports teams that are organized to compete against one another

leisure free time apart from work

macho exaggerated manliness

masculine relating to male characteristics, such as strength and aggression

media means of communication, such as television and magazines

nationalism identification with, and loyalty to, one's country

patriotism loyalty and devotion to one's country

positive deviance unethical actions, such as taking performance-enhancing drugs, that enable athletes to become more competitive or perform at a higher level

prejudice opinion decided beforehand, typically based on negative beliefs and ideas about a different social group

prestige respect and admiration based on achievement

racism judgment of other races based on prejudiced beliefs

recreation enjoyable activity undertaken for the purpose of improving health or physical fitness

regionalism devotion to local interests, such as team affiliation

rehabilitation way to learn to live with disability through training and therapy

rite formal or cermonial act often linked to religion

rugby form of football that involves tackling and handling the ball

secular not religious

socialization process that allows people to get along with other members of society by behaving in similar ways

sociologist person who studies human social behavior

sociology study and interpretation of human social behavior

specialization in sports, a process by which players develop particular strengths in controlling the game play, often resulting in more powerful but less skillful play

spectacle event meant to impress spectators

sponsorship in sports, an arrangement in which a commercial company pays to be represented by a professional athlete

stacking method of specialization that assigns positions according to race or ethnicity

stereotypical standard or accepted ideas about what a person or social group is like. These ideas are often prejudicial.

superstitious believing in the significance of irrational habits such as wearing a "lucky" pair of socks on game days

unethical relating to behavior considered morally wrong

urbanization movement of populations from rural (country) areas to urban (city) centers

white elephant in sports, an expensive, high-maintenance facility

NOTES ON SOURCES

SPORTS CULTURE AND SOCIOLOGY
(pages 4–5)

1. Howard L. Nixon II and James H. Frey, *A Sociology of Sport* (Belmont, CA: Wadsworth Publishing Company, 1996), 17.

EARLY SPORTS: FROM PLAY TO WAR
(pages 6–11)

1. Johan Huizinga, *Homo Ludens* (Boston: The Beacon Press, 1950), 2–5.
2. Nixon and Frey, *A Sociology of Sport*, 18; Eric Dunning, *Sport Matters: Sociological Studies of Sport, Violence and Civilization* (New York: Routledge, 1999), 72–79.
3. Huizinga, *Homo Ludens*, 2–5.
4. Allen Guttman, *From Ritual to Record: The Nature of Modern Sports* (New York: Columbia University Press, 1978), 3–9.
5. Studs Terkel, *Working* (New York: The New Press, 2004), 381–83.
6. Richard D. Mandell, *Sport: A Cultural History* (New York: Columbia University Press, 1984), 6.
7. Dunning, *Sport Matters*, 60.
8. BBC News, "Hunt Ban Forced Through Commons," November 19, 2004, http://news.bbc.co.uk/2/hi/uk_news/politics/4020453.stm.
9. Mandell, *Sport: A Cultural History*, 42–44.
10. Mandell, *Sport: A Cultural History*, 102.
11. Dunning, *Sport Matters*, 47–50; Guttman, *From Ritual to Record*, 24.
12. Guttman, *From Ritual to Record*, 7.
13. Dunning, *Sport Matters*, 85.
14. Les Carpenter, "NFL Orders Retreat from War Metaphors," *Washington Post*, February 1, 2009, http://www.washingtonpost.com/wp-dyn/content/article/2009/01/31/AR2009013100163.html.

THE GROWTH OF MODERN SPORTS
(pages 12–23)

1. Dunning, *Sport Matters*, 50.
2. Dunning, *Sport Matters*, 50.
3. Dunning, *Sport Matters*, 53.
4. Dunning, *Sport Matters*, 63–64.
5. Dunning, *Sport Matters*, 53.
6. Guttman, *From Ritual to Record*, 51–54.
7. Roger Bannister, *The Four-Minute Mile*, (Guilford, CT: The Lyons Press, 2004), 172.
8. Nixon and Frey, *A Sociology of Sport*, 24–28.
9. Dunning, *Sport Matters*, 97–98.
10. Nixon and Frey, *A Sociology of Sport*, 280.
11. Nixon and Frey, *A Sociology of Sport*, 38; Jorge Aranguré Jr. and Luke Cyphers, "It's Not All Sun and Games," *ESPN The Magazine*, March 13, 2009, http://sports.espn.go.com/espnmag/story?id=3974952.
12. Nixon and Frey, *A Sociology of Sport*, 49.
13. Ralph C. Wilcox, ed., *Sporting Dystopias: The Making and Meanings of Urban Sport*

Cultures (Albany, NY: State University of New York Press, 2003), 1–14.

14. Andrew Greiner, "Atlanta's Olympic Benefit Goes to the Dogs," *NBC News*, September 21, 2009, http://www.nbcchicago.com/news/local-beat/Atlantas-Olympic-Benefit-Went-to-the-Dogs-60032607.html.

15. "Louisiana Superdome Media Kit," http://www.superdome.com/uploads/media_kit_12282010.pdf.

16. Emily Mathieu, "Games Legacy: A Herd of White Elephants," *The Star*, January 30, 2010, http://www.thestar.com/business/article/757961–games-legacy-a-herd-of-white-elephants.

17. Dunning, *Sport Matters*, 50–52.

18. Dunning, *Sport Matters*, 50–59.

19. Dave Eggers, "The True Story of American Soccer," in Matt Weiland and Sean Wilsey, eds., *A Thinking Fan's Guide to the World Cup* (New York: Harper Perennial, 2006), 353–57, http://www.slate.com/id/2142554/.

20. Eduardo Galeano, *Soccer in Sun and Shadow* (New York: Verso, 1998), 171–72.

21. Eggers, "The True Story of American Soccer."

22. Norimitsu Onishi, "Japan Wrings Its Hands over Sumo's Latest Woes," *New York Times*, October 19, 2007, http://www.nytimes.com/2007/10/19/world/asia/19sumo.html; Justin McCurry, "Sumo Wrestling Hit by Match-Fixing Scandal," *The Guardian*, February 2, 2011, http://www.guardian.co.uk/world/2011/feb/02/japan-sumo-wrestling-match-fixing.

23. Eric Arnold, "Strangest Olympics Sports in History," *Forbes*, January 28, 2010, http://www.forbes.com/2010/01/28/olympics-demonstration-sports-lifestyle-sports-strangest-vancouver.html; www.insidethegames.com/olympic-sports/.

PLAYING SPORTS (pages 24–37)

1. Dunning, *Sport Matters*, 2–3.

2. Nixon and Frey, *A Sociology of Sport*, 78; Dunning, *Sport Matters*, 76–79.

3. Nixon and Frey, *A Sociology of Sport*, 103–104.

4. Nixon and Frey, *A Sociology of Sport*, 220–21.

5. Nixon and Frey, *A Sociology of Sport*, 95–96.

6. Guttman, *From Ritual to Record*, 26.

7. Michael F. Collins, "Social Exclusion from Sport and Leisure," in Barrie Houlihan, ed., *Sport & Society: A Student Introduction* (London: Sage Publications, 2003), 68–74.

8. Thorstein Veblen, *The Theory of the Leisure Class* (New York: The Modern Library, 2001), 29, 31, 188.

9. Nixon and Frey, *A Sociology of Sport*, 208–211.

10. Nixon and Frey, *A Sociology of Sport*, 25.

11. Tess Kay, "Sport and Gender," in Houlihan, *Sport & Society*, 94–101.

12. Barrie Houlihan, "Politics, Power, Policy and Sport," in Houlihan, *Sport & Society*, 41.

13. Christa Case Bryant, "Winter Olympics: Women Banned from Ski Jumping, but Women's Participation Way Up," *Christian Science Monitor*, February 22, 2010, http://www.csmonitor.com/World/Olympics/Olympics-blog/2010/0222/Winter-Olympics-Women-banned-from-ski-jumping-but-women-s-participation-way-up.

14. Amanda Ruggeri, "Why Aren't Female Ski Jumpers Allowed in the Olympics?" *Mother Jones*, February 12, 2010, http://motherjones.com/media/2010/02/did-olympic-committee-discriminate-against-female-ski-jumpers.

15. Nixon and Frey, *A Sociology of Sport*, 268–70.

16. Nixon and Frey, *A Sociology of Sport*, 254–57.

PLAYING SPORTS (pages 24–37)

17. Jere Longman, "South African Runner's Sex-Verification Result Won't Be Public," *New York Times*, November 19, 2009, http://www.nytimes.com/2009/11/20/sports/20runner.html; Christopher Clarey, "Semenya Is Back, But Acceptance Lags," *New York Times*, August 23, 2010, http://www.nytimes.com/2010/08/24/sports/24iht-ARENA.html.

18. D. Stanley Eitzen, *Fair and Foul: Beyond the Myths and Paradoxes of Sport* (Lanham, MD: Rowman & Littlefield Publishers, Inc., 2003), 93–97.

19. Nixon and Frey, *A Sociology of Sport*, 233–34.

20. Nixon and Frey, *A Sociology of Sport*, 242–48.

21. Murray Phillips and Tara Magdalinski, "Sport in Australia," in Houlihan, *Sport & Society*, 322–23.

22. Eitzen, *Fair and Foul*, 27–33; Florida State University Official Athletic Site, "Traditions," http://www.seminoles.com/trads/fsu-trads-chant.html.

23. Nixon and Frey, *A Sociology of Sport*, 222–23.

24. Paralympic.org, "Wheelchair Rugby," http://www.paralympic.org/Sport/IF_Sports/Wheelchair_Rugby/index.html.

25. Jeremy Kahn, "For Paralympians, a Bigger Field of Competition," *New York Times*, October 6, 2010, http://www.nytimes.com/2010/10/07/sports/07iht-GAMES.html.

26. Nixon and Frey, *A Sociology of Sport*, 224–25; Liz Robbins, "Getting Better with Age: Dive In," *New York Times*, August 18, 2008, http://www.nytimes.com/2008/08/21/fashion/21fitness.html; Jeff Glor, "Older Athletes Still Got Game," CBS Evening News, July 20, 2009, http://www.cbsnews.com/stories/2009/07/20/eveningnews/main5175990.shtml.

27. Dunning, *Sport Matters*, 5–6.

28. Dan Rookwood, "The Bitterest Rivalry in World Football," *The Guardian*, August 28, 2002, http://www.guardian.co.uk/football/2002/aug/28/sport.danrookwood; Barcelona vs. Real Madrid.com, "El Clasico—The Spanish Super Clasico," http://www.barcelonarealmadrid.com.

29. Tony Guadagnoll, "Harvard–Yale Rivalry a Tribute to the Student-Athlete," *ESPN SportsTravel*, October 2, 2008, http://sports.espn.go.com/travel/news/story?id=3017562.

30. Richard Evans, "Federer vs. Nadal: A Great Rivalry," *New York Times*, June 24, 2007, http://www.nytimes.com/2007/06/24/sports/24iht-SRMEN.1.6298496.html.

31. James Dart and Paolo Bandini, "Has Football Ever Started a War?" *The Guardian*, February 21, 2007, http://www.guardian.co.uk/football/2007/feb/21/theknowledge.sport.

32. George Orwell, "The Sporting Spirit," *The Collected Essays Journalism & Letters*, vol. 4, In Front of Your Nose, 1946–1950 (Boston: David R. Godine, 2000), 40–44.

33. Nixon and Frey, *A Sociology of Sport*, 289–91.

34. Mandell, *Sport: A Cultural History*, 237–46.

35. Nixon and Frey, *A Sociology of Sport*, 278; Rune-Wen Huang and Connor Gants, "Diplomacy in the Sports Arena," US-China Today, March 7, 2008, http://uschina.usc.edu/w_usct/showarticle.aspx?articleID=10957.

36. Nixon and Frey, *A Sociology of Sport*, 247; BBC Sport, "1995: Party Time for SA," September 24, 2003, http://news.bbc.co.uk/sport2/hi/rugby_union/rugby_world_cup/history/2960348.stm.

37. *The World Cup in Africa: Who Really Wins?* (New York: Disinformation, 2010).

WATCHING SPORTS (pages 38–51)

1. Dunning, *Sport Matters*, 3–6.

2. John Martin, "Federer Beats Djokovic to Reach Final," *NYTimes Straight Set Blog*, September 13, 2009, http://straightsets.blogs.nytimes.com/2009/09/13/live-analysis-federer-vs-djokovic/; www.youtube.com/watch?v=RJuEzJEQ9N4.

3. Leigh Robinson, "The Business of Sport," in Houlihan, *Sport & Society*, 173–75.

4. Nixon and Frey, *A Sociology of Sport*, 48; Anthony Crupi, "Study: Super Bowl Ad Time Soars," Mediaweek, January 18, 2011, http://www.mediaweek.com/mw/content_display/news/national-broadcast/e3i2ccbd3f8423a4c2567249ef6e69393fa.

5. Guttman, *From Ritual to Record*, 16–17.

6. Guttman, *From Ritual to Record*, 21–25.

7. Nixon and Frey, *A Sociology of Sport*, 63–67; Dunning, *Sport Matters*, 3–6.

8. Guttman, *From Ritual to Record*, 55.

9. Nixon and Frey, *A Sociology of Sport*, 76–77.

10. Guttman, *From Ritual to Record*, 11–13.

11. Ron Fimrite, "Practice Made Her Perfect," *Sports Illustrated Online*, http://sportsillustrated.cnn.com/events/1996/olympics/daily/july25/flashback.html; *CNN.com*, "Nadia Comaneci," July 7, 2008, http://www.cnn.com/2008/SPORT/04/29/nadiacomaneci/index.html.

12. David Stead, "Sport and the Media," in Houlihan, *Sport & Society*, 184–91.

13. Howard Beck, "NBA's Season of Suspense Ends," *New York Times*, July 8, 2010, http://www.nytimes.com/2010/07/09/sports/basketball/09nba.html.

14. Associated Press, "Coming to America: Beckham Will Play for MLS' L.A. Galaxy in $250M Deal," *Sports Illustrated*, January 11, 2007, http://sportsillustrated.cnn.com/2007/soccer/01/11/beckham.mls/; Catherina Elsworth, "Critics Savage Victoria Beckham's Reality Show," *The Telegraph*, July 17, 2007, http://www.telegraph.co.uk/news/world-news/1557710/Critics-savage-Victoria-Beckhams-reality-show.html.

15. Tim Arango, "Big Risk in a One-Man Brand Like Tiger Woods," *New York Times*, December 13, 2009, http://www.nytimes.com/2009/12/14/business/media/14adco.html.

16. John Branch, "As Vick Soars, Stigma of Conviction Fades," *New York Times*, November 18, 2010, http://www.nytimes.com/2010/11/19/sports/football/19vick.html.

17. Robinson in Houlihan, *Sport & Society*, 165–68.

18. Jonah Freedman, "The 50 Highest-Earning American Athletes," *Sports Illustrated.com*, 2010, http://sportsillustrated.cnn.com/specials/fortunate50-2010/index.html.

19. Freedman, "The 50 Highest-Earning American Athletes."

20. Freedman, "The 50 Highest-Earning American Athletes."

21. Eduardo Porter, "How Superstars' Pay Stifles Everyone Else," *New York Times*, December 25, 2010, http://www.nytimes.com/2010/12/26/business/26excerpt.html.

22. Eduardo Porter, "How Superstars' Pay Stifles Everyone Else."

23. Nixon and Frey, *A Sociology of Sport*, 205.

24. Dunning, *Sport Matters*, 3–6.

25. Nixon and Frey, *A Sociology of Sport*, 54–55.

26. Nixon and Frey, *A Sociology of Sport*, 113.

27. Dunning, *Sport Matters*, 59.

28. Dunning, *Sport Matters*, 56–59.

29. "Head Injuries in Football," *New York Times*, October 21, 2010, http://topics.nytimes.com/top/reference/timestopics/subjects/f/football/head_injuries/index.html.

30. Nixon and Frey, *A Sociology of Sport*, 109–110; Dunning, *Sport Matters*, 48.

31. Dunning, *Sport Matters*, 139–53.

FIND OUT MORE

Books

Bizley, Kirk. *Sport in Society (Aspects of PE)*. Chicago: Heinemann Library, 2008.

Bizley, Kirk. *Taking Part in Sport (Aspects of PE)*. Chicago: Heinemann Library, 2008.

Fleder, Rob. *Fifty Years of Great Writing: Sports Illustrated, 1954–2004*. New York: Sports Illustrated, 2004.

Gifford, Clive. *Athletics (Great Sporting Events)*. London, UK: Franklin Watts, 2011.

Kerr, Jim. *Sports (Media Power)*. Mankato, Minn.: Amicus, 2010.

Remnick, David, ed. *The Only Game in Town: Sportswriting from The New Yorker*. New York: Random House, 2010.

Stevenson, Matthew Mills, and Michael Martin, eds. *Rules of the Game: The Best Sports Writing from Harper's Magazine*. New York: Franklin Square, 2010.

Weiland, Matt, and Sean Wilsey, eds. *A Thinking Fan's Guide to the World Cup*. New York: Harper Perennial, 2006.

DVDs

Eight Men Out (Santa Monica, Calif.: MGM Home Entertainment, 1988; reissued 2001).
This drama tells the story of the infamous "Black Sox" scandal, when members of the Chicago White Sox accepted bribes to throw the 1919 World Series.

Friday Night Lights (Universal City, Calif.: Universal, 2004).
This drama about football culture in a small, fictional Texas town explores issues of race, disability, regionalism, and the many ways sports culture is tied to social identity.

Hoop Dreams (Irvington, N.Y.: Criterion Collection, 2005; film originally released 1994).
This documentary follows two African-American high-school basketball players in Chicago over the course of five years, as they deal with the pressures of college recruitment.

Murderball (New York: Lions Gate Entertainment, 2005).
This documentary about wheelchair rugby focuses on the rivalry between the U.S. and Canadian teams as they prepare for the 2004 Paralympic Games.

Unforgivable Blackness: The Rise and Fall of Jack Johnson (Alexandria, Va.: PBS Home Video, 2005).
This biographical documentary by Ken Burns tells the story of Jack Johnson, who was the first African-American world heavyweight-boxing champion and an early sports celebrity.

The World Cup in Africa: Who Really Wins? (New York: Disinformation, 2010).
This documentary examines the positive and negative effects of the 2010 soccer World Cup on South African society.

Websites

There are also many resources online for learning about sports culture:

http://espn.go.com
The Entertainment and Sports Programming Network's (ESPN) news site covers games and sporting events from all over the world.

www.olympic.org
The International Olympic Committee's website has a wealth of information about the Olympics.

www.livestrong.com/sports-and-recreation
Cyclist Lance Armstrong's Livestrong website is a resource for learning about different sports and recreational activities, as well as how to stay healthy and fit.

www.fifa.com
This is the website of soccer's governing body.

INDEX